Some Kids Wear Leg Braces

by Lola M. Schaefer

Consulting Editor: Gail Saunders-Smith, Ph.D.

Consultant: Lawrence Z. Stern, M.D.
Medical Consultant, Muscular Dystrophy Association
Professor of Neurology, University of Arizona

Pebble Books

an imprint of Capstone Press
Mankato, Minnesota

Pebble Books are published by Capstone Press
151 Good Counsel Drive, P.O. Box 669, Mankato, Minnesota 56002
http://www.capstone-press.com

1 2 3 4 5 6 06 05 04 03 02 01

Library of Congress Cataloging-in-Publication Data
Schaefer, Lola M., 1950–
    Some kids wear leg braces/by Lola M. Schaefer.
    p. cm.—(Understanding differences)
    Includes bibliographical references and index.
    Summary: Describes some of the reasons children might be required to wear leg
braces and how they are helpful.
    ISBN 0-7368-0667-9
    1. Physically handicapped—Juvenile literature. 2. Orthopedic braces—Juvenile
literature. 3. Leg—Abnormalities—Juvenile literature. [1. Orthopedic braces. 2. Leg.
3. Physically handicapped.] I. Title. II. Series.
HV3011 .S35 2001
362.4′3—dc21   00-024443

Note to Parents and Teachers

The Understanding Differences series supports national social
studies standards related to individual development and identity.
This book describes and illustrates the special needs of children
who wear leg braces. The photographs support early readers in
understanding the text. The repetition of words and phrases helps
early readers learn new words. This book also introduces early
readers to subject-specific vocabulary words, which are defined in
the Words to Know section. Early readers may need assistance to
read some words and to use the Table of Contents, Words to
Know, Read More, Internet Sites, and Index/Word List sections
of the book.

Table of Contents

Some kids wear leg braces. Leg braces help support legs that are weak or injured.

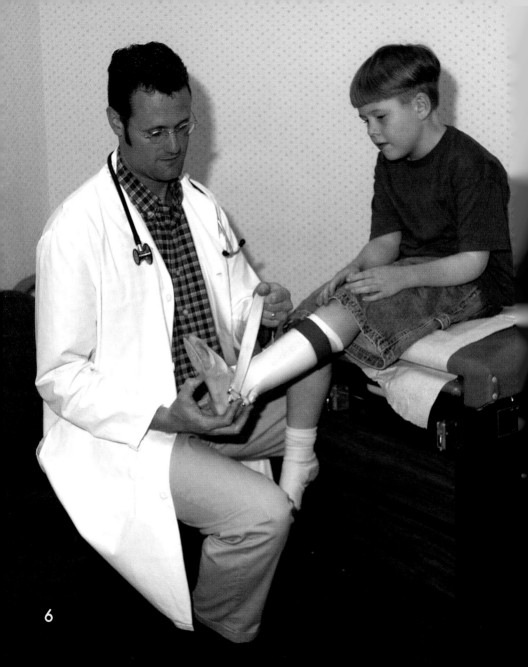

Some kids wear leg braces because their muscles or bones did not grow right. Other kids wear leg braces because they were injured.

Physical therapists teach kids how to use leg braces. They teach kids how to exercise and move.

Leg braces sometimes cover only a small part of a leg. They sometimes cover almost all of a leg.

Kids who wear leg braces
sometimes use crutches
or walkers. They can
go for walks.

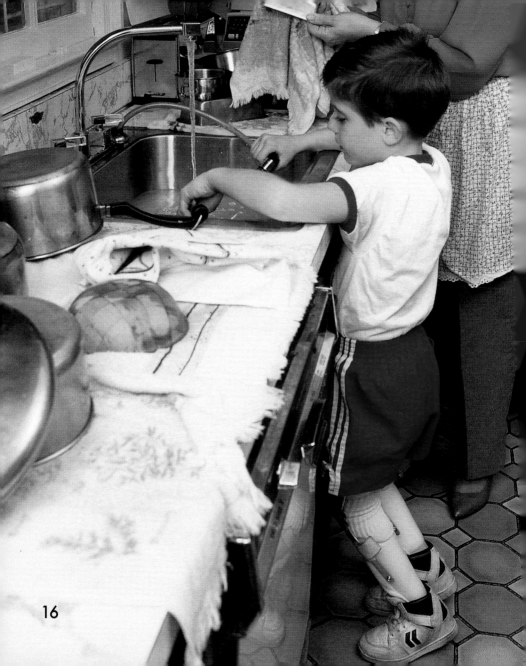

Kids who wear leg braces help others. They do jobs at home.

Kids who wear leg braces like to have fun. They play games with their friends.

Kids who wear leg braces enjoy animals. They take care of their pets.

Words to Know

crutch—a long wooden or metal stick with a padded top; people with leg injuries often use crutches to help them walk.

exercise—physical activity that a person does to keep fit and healthy

injured—damaged or harmed; some people wear leg braces because they were injured.

physical therapist—a person trained to give treatment to people who are ill, injured, or have physical disabilities; massage and exercise are two kinds of treatment.

support—to give assistance or help hold another thing in place; leg braces support weak joints and injured legs and feet.

walker—a metal frame with four legs that gives support to people when they walk; walkers improve balance and stability.

Read More

Bergman, Thomas. *Precious Time: Children Living with Muscular Dystrophy.* Don't Turn Away. Milwaukee: Gareth Stevens, 1996.

Dobkin, Bonnie. *Just A Little Different.* A Rookie Reader. New York: Children's Press, 1994.

Dwight, Laura. *We Can Do It!* New York: Star Bright Books, 1997.

Internet Sites

Cerebral Palsy
http://www.med.virginia.edu/cmc/tutorials/cp/index.html

Everybody's Different, Nobody's Perfect
http://www.mdausa.org/publications/nobody/index.html

Seeing Differences: Cerebral Palsy
http://tqjunior.advanced.org/5852/cphome.htm

Index/Word List

Word Count: 144
Early-Intervention Level: 9

Editorial Credits
Mari C. Schuh, editor; Kia Bielke, designer; Katy Kudela, photo researcher

Photo Credits
Gregg R. Andersen, cover, 6, 8, 10, 18
International Stock/George Ancona, 16
Jerry Ruff, 14
Muscular Dystrophy Association, 1, 4, 20
Ron Chapple/FPG International LLC, 12

Special thanks to the children and staff of Pediatric Therapy Services in Mankato, Minnesota, NOW CARE Medical Center in Mankato, Minnesota, and Coulee Children's Center in La Crosse, Wisconsin, for their assistance with this book.